LET'S LEARN TO THE QURA

Level 4

With Diagrams and Notes for Teachers and Parents

Let's Learn to Read the Quran - Level 4
6th Edition (New Edition)

Published by **INVITATION PUBLISHING**

Jan 2024

The Glade Business Centre
Unit 13, Forum Road
Nottingham, NG5 9RW

0115 8550961
info@invitationpublishing.co.uk
www.invitationpublishing.co.uk

©Invitation Publishing 2024

All rights reserved. No part of this publication may be reproduced, stored in retrieval system, or transmitted, in any form or by any means, electronic, mechanical, photocopying, recording or otherwise, without the prior written permission of the copyright owner.

Instructions For Teachers and Parents
"The best amongst you is the one who learns and then teaches the Quran"

The Majestic Quran is the speech of Allah Almighty; these are divine words revealed to the last messenger Muhammad ﷺ in clear and beautiful Arabic. The Quranic verses are melodious and rhythmic yet they are not poetry. Muslims must learn to read the divine revelation in its original Arabic language. Parents in the past as well as today throughout the Muslim world were, and are eager to teach their five and six year old children to read the Quran.

The benefits and merits of reading the Quran are enormous; the Prophet ﷺ said there are ten merits for reading each letter of the Quran and alif-lamm-meem are three letters, their reward is thirty merits. On another occasion he said "a person who doesn't know anything from the Quran is like a derelict house" (Tirmizi).

This manual has been written for beginners, it will be useful for all age's even children as young as five or six will be able to use it (Insha-Allah). With guidance from teachers and parents these principles of Quran reading can be mastered in a short period of time.

It is important for the English speaking learner to familiarise themselves with the Arabic script so that they can pronounce the syllables and then make words without having to look at the transliteration. The transliteration should be used to counter check doubts in pronunciation. If the rules of reading are properly learnt and thoroughly practiced by doing all the exercise then the pupil will begin to read the Quran very quickly.

Throughout this manual the focus has been on developing both the phonological awareness and the mental resource bank of known words. Although some children will prefer one than the other in learning to read, nevertheless both methods are useful. By taking this structured approach in both methods children will learn quickly.

Acknowledgments:
This manual is based on three very famous manuals;
Yassarn-Al-Quran by Qari Muhammad Ismael
Noorani Qaida by Qari Noor Muhammad
Ahsan-ul-Qawaid by Qari Shamsuddin Barudwi
May Allah bless the soul of these teachers of the glorious Quran.

CONTENTS

Arabic letters and English equivalents	1
Articulation of the Arabic letters (Makharij)	2
The signs of Waqf	3
The most common words in the Quran	5
The most common phrases in the Quran	8
Prayers for day and night	12
Morale boosting phrases	15
Adhan	17
How to perform the Salah	19
The Muslim creed	24
The six holy words	25
20 glorious Surahs of the Quran	28

بِسْمِ اللهِ الرَّحْمٰنِ الرَّحِيمِ

ARABIC LETTERS AND ENGLISH EQUIVALENTS

1. The Arabic language is read from right to left.
2. The letter 'Ain' has no equivalent in English, Hence, it is translated with an asper (').

#	Eng	Arabic Name	Letter	#	Eng	Arabic Name	Letter
1.	A, U, I	Alif	ا	16.	T	Tuaa	ط
2.	B	Baa	ب	17.	Z	Zhuaa	ظ
3.	T	Taa	ت	18.	'	Ain	ع
4.	Th	Thaa	ث	19.	Gh	Ghain	غ
5.	J	Jeem	ج	20.	F	Faa	ف
6.	H	Hhaa	ح	21.	Q	Qaaf	ق
7.	Kh	Khaa	خ	22.	K	Kaaf	ك
8.	D	Daal	د	23.	L	Laam	ل
9.	Dh	Dhaal	ذ	24.	M	Meem	م
10.	R	Raa	ر	25.	N	Noon	ن
11.	Z	Zaa	ز	26.	H	Haa	ه
12.	S	Seen	س	27.	W	Waw	و
13.	Sh	Sheen	ش	28.	'	Hamzah	ء
14.	S	Suaad	ص	29.	J	Yaa	ي
15.	D	Dhuaad	ض				

ARTICULATION OF THE ARABIC LETTERS

For correct pronunciation the sound of each letter must originate from the correct parts of the mouth and with the correct quality (i.e. Soft, Hard, Sharp etc.). Fourteen places can be identified from where the 29 letters are sounded (see diagram below).

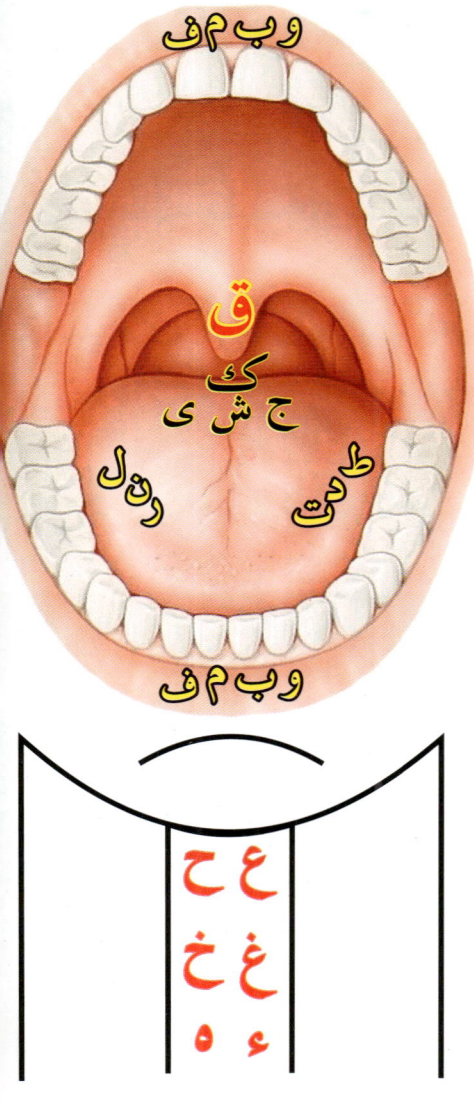

Bottom of throat Glottal:	ء ه
Middle of Throat Phyrnaged:	ح ع
Top of Throat	خ غ
Far Back of Mouth Extreme Back of Tongue Touches Soft Palate	ق
Back of Tongue Touches Hard Palate	ك
Middle of Tongue Touches Roof of Mouth	ى ش ج
Side of Tongue Touches Gums from Pre-Molars to Molars	ض
Tip of Tongue Touches Gums from Pre-Molars to Incisor	ر ن ل
Tip of Tongue Touches Roots of Upper Incisor	ت د ط
Tip of Tongue Strikes the Upper Edge of the Incisor	ذ ظ ث
Tip of Tongue The Root of the Lower Incisor	ص س ز
Lips	ف م ب و

THE SIGNS OF WAQF (PAUSE)

◯ This symbol is equivalent to a full stop in English.

قُلْ هُوَ اللّٰهُ أَحَدٌ ◯

صلے This is a symbol of continue to read, don't stop.

وَإِن يَمْسَسْكَ اللَّهُ بِضُرٍّ فَلَا كَاشِفَ لَهُ إِلَّا هُوَ ۖ وَإِن يَمْسَسْكَ بِخَيْرٍ فَهُوَ عَلَىٰ كُلِّ شَيْءٍ قَدِيرٌ ◯

قلے This symbol means it is better to stop but you are allowed to continue.

قُل رَّبِّي أَعْلَمُ بِعِدَّتِهِم مَّا يَعْلَمُهُمْ إِلَّا قَلِيلٌ ۗ فَلَا تُمَارِ فِيهِمْ إِلَّا مِرَاءً ظَاهِرًا

∴ This symbol comes as a pair and you are allowed to stop at any one but not at both.

ذَٰلِكَ الْكِتَابُ لَا رَيْبَ ۛ فِيهِ ۛ هُدًى لِّلْمُتَّقِينَ

قف This symbol means it is better to stop and take a fresh breath but you can continue if you want.

وَإِذْ أَخَذْنَا مِيثَاقَ بَنِي إِسْرَائِيلَ لَا تَعْبُدُونَ إِلَّا اللَّهَ وَبِالْوَالِدَيْنِ إِحْسَانًا

THE SIGNS OF WAQF (PAUSE)

س — This symbol means pause here. Pause the sound for a moment without breaking breath.

وَقِيلَ مَنْ سٓ رَاقٍ

م — This symbol means it is a compulsory stop, otherwise the meaning is changed.

إِنَّمَا يَسْتَجِيبُ الَّذِينَ يَسْمَعُونَۗ وَالْمَوْتَىٰ يَبْعَثُهُمُ اللَّهُ ثُمَّ إِلَيْهِ يُرْجَعُونَ

لا — This symbol means "prohibited stop", do not stop here.

اَلَّذِينَ تَتَوَفَّاهُمُ الْمَلَائِكَةُ طَيِّبِينَ ۙ يَقُولُونَ سَلَامٌ عَلَيْكُمُ ادْخُلُوا الْجَنَّةَ بِمَا كُنتُمْ تَعْمَلُونَ

ج — This symbol means "permissible stop", you may either stop or carry on reading.

نَحْنُ نَقُصُّ عَلَيْكَ نَبَأَهُم بِالْحَقِّ ۚ إِنَّهُمْ فِتْيَةٌ آمَنُوا بِرَبِّهِمْ وَزِدْنَاهُمْ هُدًى

ط — This symbol means it is necessary to stop here.

وَنَحْنُ نُسَبِّحُ بِحَمْدِكَ وَنُقَدِّسُ لَكَ ۖ قَالَ إِنِّي أَعْلَمُ مَا لَا تَعْلَمُونَ

THE MOST COMMON WORDS IN THE QURAN

These are the most-repeated Quranic words. Pupils must master them before starting to read the Quran. These words should form the mental resource bank of known words by the pupils. You should be able to read the whole line in one breath, then two lines etc.

بِهِ	كُنْتُمْ	اَلصَّلٰوةُ	اَللّٰهُ
رَبَّكُمْ	أَقِيْمُوا	رَبُّ	اَلزَّكٰوةُ
إِلَّا	قُلْ	اتُوْا	بَعْدَ
رَسُوْلُ	فِيْهَا	قَالُوْا	رَحْمٰنُ
ثُمَّ	مُفْلِحُوْنَ	أَنْتُمْ	قَالَ
عَذَابُ	أَنْفُسَكُمْ	قُلُوْبُ	فَإِذَا
بِمَا	كَانُوْا	ذٰلِكَ	كَانَ
اَلْأَرْضُ	سَمِيْعُ	عَلِيْمُ	عَظِيْمُ

THE MOST COMMON WORDS IN THE QURAN

سَمٰوٰتٌ	مَعَ	مُصْلِحُوْنَ	يَشْعُرُوْنَ
فَرَقْنَا	اٰيٰتٌ	يَوْمًا	إِنَّمَا
رَزَقْنَا	أَخْرَجَ	مِنْكُمْ	مَاءٌ
أَمَرَ	مِنْهُ	أَرَادَ	إِنَّا
عَمَّ	دِيْنٌ	عِنْدَ	أَجْرُهُمْ
وَلَا	عَلٰى	هٰذَا	لَنَا
كَافِرِيْنَ	وَمَا	مَنْ	كَافِرُوْنَ
عَلَيْهِ	أَلَمْ	فَمَا	إِلٰى
اٰمَنُوْا	عَلَيْهِمْ	كُنَّا	مَعَهُمْ

THE MOST COMMON WORDS IN THE QURAN

نَارٌ	كَفَرُوا	لَا	لَعَلَّكُمْ
الَّذِينَ	جَنَّتُ	يَشَآءُ	الَّذِى
دُونَ	أَنْزَلَ	النَّاسُ	جَآءَ
كَذِبٌ	شَىْءٌ	أُولَٰئِكَ	الْيَوْمَ
إِذَا	كَذَّبَ	كُلُّ	إِنَّ
أَنْتَ	يَعْلَمُونَ	قَوْمٌ	قَبْلُ
يَعْلَمُ	هُوَ	فِى	ظَلَمُوا
لَكُمْ	جَعَلْنَا	هُدًى	لَهُمْ
	وَ	مِنْ	مَا

7

THE MOST COMMON PHRASES IN THE QURAN

1. Pupils are expected to read each line without stuttering.
2. Read each line in one breath.
3. Then 2 lines in one breath.

IN PRAISE OF ALLAH:

And He knows everything	وَهُوَ بِكُلِّ شَىْءٍ عَلِيمٌ
Indeed, you are wise, the all knowing	إِنَّكَ أَنْتَ الْعَلِيمُ الْحَكِيمُ
Indeed, you are the hearer, the all knowing	إِنَّكَ أَنْتَ السَّمِيعُ الْعَلِيمُ
Indeed, you are the strong, the wise	إِنَّكَ أَنْتَ الْعَزِيزُ الْحَكِيمُ
Indeed, Allah is kind and caring to people	إِنَّ اللهَ بِالنَّاسِ لَرَؤُوفٌ رَحِيمٌ
And He is the hearer and the knower	وَهُوَ السَّمِيعُ الْعَلِيمُ
Indeed, Allah is forgiving, merciful	إِنَّ اللهَ غَفُورٌ رَحِيمٌ
And indeed, Allah is appreciative, knower	فَإِنَّ اللهَ شَاكِرٌ عَلِيمٌ

Indeed, Allah has control over everything	إِنَّ اللّهَ عَلَى كُلِّ شَيْءٍ قَدِيرٌ
And Allah is quick to reckon	وَاللّهُ سَرِيعُ الْحِسَابِ
And Allah is compassionate with the people	وَاللّهُ رَءُوفٌ بِالْعِبَادِ
Indeed, Allah sees whatever you are doing	إِنَّ اللّهَ بِمَا تَعْمَلُونَ بَصِيرٌ
And Allah is aware of whatever you are doing	وَاللّهُ بِمَا تَعْمَلُونَ خَبِيرٌ
And He is the exalted, the mighty	وَهُوَ الْعَلِيُّ الْعَظِيمُ
And Allah is self-sufficient, gentle	وَاللّهُ غَنِيٌّ حَلِيمٌ
And know that Allah is self-sufficient, praiseworthy	وَاعْلَمُوا أَنَّ اللّهَ غَنِيٌّ حَمِيدٌ
And Allah sustains whoever he wills without limits	وَاللّهُ يَرْزُقُ مَن يَشَاءُ بِغَيْرِ حِسَابٍ
And Allah's grace on you is abundant	وَكَانَ فَضْلُ اللّهِ عَلَيْكَ عَظِيمًا

Indeed, Allah is keeping a watch on you	إِنَّ اللهَ كَانَ عَلَيْكُمْ رَقِيبًا
And Allah is sufficient as a reckoner	وَكَفَى بِاللهِ حَسِيبًا
Indeed, Allah is forgiving, merciful	إِنَّ اللهَ كَانَ تَوَّابًا رَّحِيمًا
Indeed, Allah is very kind to you	إِنَّ اللهَ كَانَ بِكُمْ رَحِيمًا
Indeed, Allah is most high, great	إِنَّ اللهَ كَانَ عَلِيًّا كَبِيرًا
Indeed, Allah is a witness of all things	إِنَّ اللهَ كَانَ عَلَى كُلِّ شَيْءٍ شَهِيدًا
And Allah is sufficient as a witness	وَكَفَى بِاللهِ شَهِيدًا
And Allah is sufficient as a guardian	وَكَفَى بِاللهِ وَكِيلًا
Indeed, Allah is the reckoner of all things	إِنَّ اللهَ كَانَ عَلَى كُلِّ شَيْءٍ حَسِيبًا
And Allah is strong, wise	وَكَانَ اللهُ عَزِيزًا حَكِيمًا

IN PRAISE OF BELIEVERS:

And give good news to the believers	وَبَشِّرِ الْمُؤْمِنِينَ
Indeed, the help of Allah is near	أَلَا إِنَّ نَصْرَ اللهِ قَرِيبٌ
And they are the God fearing	وَأُولَٰئِكَ هُمُ الْمُتَّقُونَ
And they will have no fear	وَلَا خَوْفٌ عَلَيْهِمْ
And they will have no grief	وَلَا هُمْ يَحْزَنُونَ
Indeed, Allah is with the patient	إِنَّ اللهَ مَعَ الصَّابِرِينَ
Indeed, Allah loves those who repent	إِنَّ اللهَ يُحِبُّ التَّوَّابِينَ
And he loves the pure	وَيُحِبُّ الْمُتَطَهِّرِينَ
And they will live there (paradise) forever	وَهُمْ فِيهَا خَالِدُونَ
Indeed, in that is a sign for the believers	إِنَّ فِي ذَٰلِكَ لَآيَةً لِلْمُؤْمِنِينَ

PRAYERS FOR DAY AND NIGHT

Memorise them and remember to read them at the appropriate times

When you wake up:

اَلْحَمْدُ لِلّٰهِ الَّذِىْ أَحْيَانَا بَعْدَ مَا أَمَاتَنَا وَ إِلَيْهِ النُّشُوْرُ

All Praise is due to Allah who has arisen us after death and to Him is our assembly.

When going to sleep (lay on your right side):

بِاسْمِكَ اللّٰهُمَّ أَمُوْتُ وَأَحْيَا

By your name (Allah) I live and I die.

When beginning a meal (after washing your hands):

بِسْمِ اللهِ وَعَلٰى بَرَكَةِ اللهِ

I begin with the name of Allah ﷻ and with His blessings.

When you forget to say Dua at the start and remember during the meal:

بِسْمِ اللهِ أَوَّلَهُ وَاٰخِرَهُ

In the name of Allah, from start to end.

PRAYERS FOR DAY AND NIGHT

After eating your meal:

اَلْحَمْدُ لِلّٰهِ الَّذِىْ اَطْعَمَنَا وَسَقَانَا وَجَعَلَنَا مِنَ الْمُسْلِمِيْنَ

All praise is for Allah who fed us and gave us to drink and made us amongst the Muslims.

When you are travelling:

سُبْحٰنَ الَّذِىْ سَخَّرَ لَنَا هٰذَا وَمَا كُنَّا لَهُ مُقْرِنِيْنَ وَإِنَّا إِلٰى رَبِّنَا لَمُنْقَلِبُوْنَ

Glory be to Him who made this controllable for us otherwise we were not capable of it and we will be returning to our Benevolent Lord.

When entering your home:

اَللّٰهُمَّ إِنِّىْ أَسْئَلُكَ خَيْرَ الْمَوْلِجِ وَخَيْرَ الْمَخْرَجِ

O Lord! I seek from You the best place to enter and the best place to leave.

When leaving your home:

بِسْمِ اللهِ تَوَكَّلْتُ عَلَى اللهِ لَاحَوْلَ وَلَاقُوَّةَ إِلَّا بِاللهِ الْعَلِىِّ الْعَظِيْمِ

In the name of Allah, upon Him I rely, I have no ability or power except that from Allah the Exalted, the Mighty.

PRAYERS FOR DAY AND NIGHT

When looking into the mirror:

اَللّٰهُمَّ أَنْتَ حَسَّنْتَ خَلْقِىْ فَحَسِّنْ خُلُقِىْ

O Lord! Just as you created me beautifully so make my character beautiful

For protection against harm:

بِسْمِ اللهِ الَّذِىْ لَا يَضُرُّ مَعَ اسْمِهٖ شَىْءٌ فِى الْأَرْضِ وَلَا فِى السَّمَاءِ وَهُوَ السَّمِيْعُ الْعَلِيْمُ

In the name of Allah and by the greatness of His name nothing on earth and the heavens can harm and He is the all listening and all Knowing.

When entering the toilet (with the left foot):

اَللّٰهُمَّ إِنِّىْ أَعُوْذُ بِكَ مِنَ الْخُبْثِ وَالْخَبَائِثِ

O Lord, I seek Your refuge from all wicked things.

When leaving the toilet (with the right foot):

اَلْحَمْدُ لِلّٰهِ الَّذِىْ أَذْهَبَ عَنِّى الْأَذٰى وَعَافَانِىْ

All praises is for Allah who has removed harm from me and given me relief

MORALE BOOSTING PHRASES

To greet each other

| Peace be upon you and Allah's mercy | اَلسَّلَامُ عَلَيْكُمْ وَرَحْمَةُاللهِ |

To express joy and surprise

| Whatever Allah wished | مَاشَآءَاللهُ |

To express hope for the future

| If Allah willed | إِنْ شَآءَاللهُ |

Upon hearing good news

| Glory be to Allah | سُبْحَانَاللهِ |

To thank Allah

| All praises are for Allah | اَلْحَمْدُلِلّٰهِ |

When receiving something

| May Allah reward you | جَزَاكَ اللهُ |

A prayer for a fellow Muslim

| May Allah have mercy on you | يَرْحَمُكَ اللهُ |

MORALE BOOSTING PHRASES

A prayer for a fellow non-Muslim

| May Allah guide you | يَهْدِيكُمُ اللهُ |

To seek forgiveness

| I seek Allah's forgiveness | أَسْتَغْفِرُ اللهَ |

Upon hearing sad news

| To Allah we belong and to Him we return | إِنَّا لِلَّهِ وَإِنَّا إِلَيْهِ رَاجِعُونَ |

When you have decided to do something

| Allah is sufficient for me and the best Protector | حَسْبِيَ اللهُ وَنِعْمَ الْوَكِيلُ |

When you see someone laughing

| May Allah keep you laughing all of your life | أَضْحَكَ اللهُ سِنَّكَ |

When you like someone

| I love you for Allah's sake | إِنِّى أُحِبُّكَ فِى اللهِ |

When you have evil thoughts

| I seek Allah's protection from the rejected devil | أَعُوذُ بِاللهِ مِنَ الشَّيْطَنِ الرَّجِيمِ |

THE ADHAN

اَللهُ أَكْبَرُ اَللهُ أَكْبَرُ   اَللهُ أَكْبَرُ اَللهُ أَكْبَرُ

أَشْهَدُ أَنْ لَآ إِلٰهَ إِلَّااللهُ   أَشْهَدُ أَنْ لَآ إِلٰهَ إِلَّااللهُ

أَشْهَدُ أَنَّ مُحَمَّدًا رَّسُوْلُ اللهِ   أَشْهَدُ أَنَّ مُحَمَّدًا رَّسُوْلُ اللهِ

حَيَّ عَلَى الصَّلٰوةِ   حَيَّ عَلَى الصَّلٰوةِ

حَيَّ عَلَى الْفَلَاحِ   حَيَّ عَلَى الْفَلَاحِ

اَللهُ أَكْبَرُ   اَللهُ أَكْبَرُ

لَآ إِلٰهَ إِلَّا اللهُ

For the Fajr Adhan, add the following words after حَيَّ عَلَى الْفَلَاحِ

اَلصَّلٰوةُ خَيْرٌ مِّنَ النَّوْمِ   اَلصَّلٰوةُ خَيْرٌ مِّنَ النَّوْمِ

Iqamah: Before starting the congregational prayer, add these words to the adhan after حَيَّ عَلَى الْفَلَاحِ

قَدْ قَامَتِ الصَّلٰوةُ   قَدْ قَامَتِ الصَّلٰوةُ

THE ADHAN

Translation of the Adhan

Allah is the Greatest, Allah is the Greatest
Allah is the Greatest, Allah is the Greatest
I bear witness that there is no God but Allah
I bear witness that there is no God but Allah
I bear witness that Muhammad is the Messenger of Allah
I bear witness that Muhammad is the Messenger of Allah
Come to prayer, Come to prayer
Come to success, Come to success
Allah is the Greatest, Allah is the Greatest
There is no God but Allah

The Prayer After the Adhan

اَللّٰهُمَّ رَبَّ هٰذِهِ الدَّعْوَةِ التَّامَّةِ وَالصَّلٰوةِ الْقَائِمَةِ اٰتِ مُحَمَّدَ الْوَسِيْلَةَ وَالْفَضِيْلَةَ وَالدَّرَجَةَ الرَّفِيْعَةَ وَابْعَثْهُ مَقَامًا مَّحْمُوْدَ الَّذِىْ وَعَدْتَّهُ وَارْزُقْنَا شَفَاعَتَهُ يَوْمَ الْقِيٰمَةِ إِنَّكَ لَاتُخْلِفُ الْمِيْعَاد

O Lord, the Master of this perfect call and of the proper prayer, grant our leader Muhammad ﷺ the rank of Wasilah and Fadilah (high station of virtue) and appoint him to the rank of Mahmood, the one that You have promised, grant us his intercession, certainly You do not break promises.

HOW TO PERFORM THE SALAH

In order to perform the prayer, the following words and passages must be memorised:

At Takbeer-At-Tehreemah

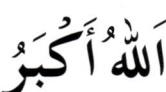 Allah is the Greatest

The Thana

سُبْحَانَكَ اللّٰهُمَّ وَبِحَمْدِكَ وَتَبَارَكَ
اسْمُكَ وَتَعَالٰى جَدُّكَ وَلَآ إِلٰهَ غَيْرُكَ

Glory be to You O Allah, all praise is for You, blessed is Your name and exalted is Your Majesty. There is no god other than You.

Taawudh

أَعُوذُ بِاللهِ مِنَ الشَّيْطٰنِ الرَّجِيمِ

I seek refuge in Allah from the rejected devil

Basmallah

بِسْمِ اللهِ الرَّحْمٰنِ الرَّحِيمِ

In the name of Allah the Kind, the Caring.

HOW TO PERFORM THE SALAH

Fatihah

اَلْحَمْدُ لِلّٰهِ رَبِّ الْعٰلَمِيْنَ ۞ اَلرَّحْمٰنِ الرَّحِيْمِ ۞ مٰلِكِ يَوْمِ الدِّيْنِ ۞ إِيَّاكَ نَعْبُدُ وَإِيَّاكَ نَسْتَعِيْنُ ۞ اِهْدِنَا الصِّرَاطَ الْمُسْتَقِيْمَ ۞ صِرَاطَ الَّذِيْنَ أَنْعَمْتَ عَلَيْهِمْ ۙ غَيْرِ الْمَغْضُوْبِ عَلَيْهِمْ وَلَا الضَّآلِّيْنَ ۞ (آمين)

All praises are for Allah, the Lord of the worlds. The Kind, the Caring, the Master of Judgement Day. We worship You alone and from You alone we seek help. Guide us on the straight path, the path of those You favoured, not those who are condemned nor the misguided ones.

Then recite any Surah after this

For Example:

قُلْ هُوَ اللَّهُ أَحَدٌ ۞ اللَّهُ الصَّمَدُ ۞ لَمْ يَلِدْ وَلَمْ يُولَدْ ۞ وَلَمْ يَكُنْ لَهُ كُفُوًا أَحَدٌ ۞

He is Allah, the One, Allah the Eternal. He is not a father nor a son. None is equal to Him.

HOW TO PERFORM THE SALAH

اَللّٰهُ اَكْبَرُ Allah is the Greatest

Tasbeeh

Bow down and say, placing your hands on your knees:

Glorified is my Lord, the most High (Three times) سُبْحَانَ رَبِّيَ الْعَظِيْمِ

Hamd

سَمِعَ اللّٰهُ لِمَنْ حَمِدَهُ رَبَّنَا لَكَ الْحَمْدُ

Allah has heard him who praises Him. O our Lord! All praise is for You.

اَللّٰهُ اَكْبَرُ Allah is the Greatest

At-Tasbeeh As-Sajda

Then go into the prostration and say:

Glorified is my Lord the Almighty (Three times) سُبْحَانَ رَبِّيَ الْأَعْلٰى

While sitting up say:

اَللّٰهُ اَكْبَرُ Allah is the Greatest

Repeat second Sajdah the same way by saying:

اَللّٰهُ اَكْبَرُ Allah is the Greatest

Stand up again for second Rakah. Recite Fatihah and any other Surah (not repeating the first one).

Then go into Ruku, stand up, perform Sajdah 1, sit up and Sajdah 2 then remain seated.

HOW TO PERFORM THE SALAH

Tashahud

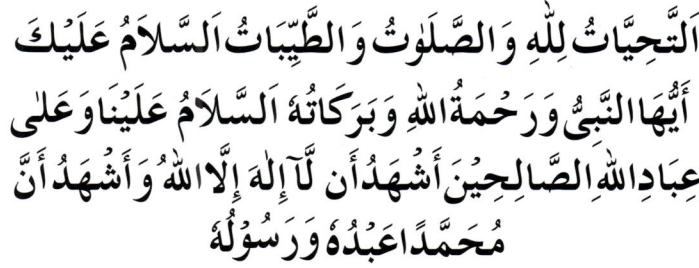

اَلتَّحِيَّاتُ لِلّٰهِ وَالصَّلَوٰتُ وَالطَّيِّبَاتُ اَلسَّلَامُ عَلَيْكَ أَيُّهَا النَّبِىُّ وَرَحْمَةُ اللّٰهِ وَبَرَكَاتُهٗ اَلسَّلَامُ عَلَيْنَا وَعَلٰى عِبَادِ اللّٰهِ الصَّالِحِيْنَ أَشْهَدُ أَنْ لَّا إِلٰهَ إِلَّا اللّٰهُ وَأَشْهَدُ أَنَّ مُحَمَّدًا عَبْدُهٗ وَرَسُوْلُهٗ

All verbal praises, bodily devotions and charity are for Allah. Peace be upon you, O Prophet and Allah's mercy and His blessings. Peace be on us all and on the righteous servants of Allah. I bear witness that there is no god except Allah and I bear witness that Muhammad is His servant and Messenger.

The Darood

اَللّٰهُمَّ صَلِّ عَلٰى مُحَمَّدٍ وَّعَلٰى اٰلِ مُحَمَّدٍ كَمَا صَلَّيْتَ عَلٰى اِبْرَاهِيْمَ وَعَلٰى اٰلِ اِبْرَاهِيْمَ إِنَّكَ حَمِيْدٌ مَّجِيْدٌ اَللّٰهُمَّ بَارِكْ عَلٰى مُحَمَّدٍ وَّعَلٰى اٰلِ مُحَمَّدٍ كَمَا بَارَكْتَ عَلٰى اِبْرَاهِيْمَ وَعَلٰى اٰلِ اِبْرَاهِيْمَ إِنَّكَ حَمِيْدٌ مَّجِيْدٌ

O Allah! Exalt Muhammad and exalt the family of Muhammad as you exalted Ibrahim and the family of Ibrahim. Surely You are the praiseworthy and most Glorious. O Allah! Bless Muhammad and bless the family of Muhammad as You blessed Ibrahim and the family of Ibrahim. Surely You are praiseworthy and the most Glorious.

HOW TO PERFORM THE SALAH

Dua

رَبِّ اجْعَلْنِيْ مُقِيْمَ الصَّلٰوةِ وَمِنْ ذُرِّيَّتِيْ ۖ رَبَّنَا وَتَقَبَّلْ دُعَآءِ ۚ رَبَّنَا اغْفِرْلِيْ وَلِوَالِدَيَّ وَلِلْمُؤْمِنِيْنَ يَوْمَ يَقُوْمُ الْحِسَابُ

O My Lord! Make me and my children regular in prayer. Our Lord accept the prayer. Our Lord forgive me, my parents and all the believers on the Day of Judgement.

Salam

اَلسَّلَامُ عَلَيْكُمْ وَرَحْمَةُ اللهِ

Say Salam by turning you head towards the right shoulder and then towards the left shoulder.

Dua Qanoot

اَللّٰهُمَّ إِنَّا نَسْتَعِيْنُكَ وَنَسْتَغْفِرُكَ وَنُؤْمِنُ بِكَ وَنَتَوَكَّلُ عَلَيْكَ وَنُثْنِيْ عَلَيْكَ الْخَيْرَ وَنَشْكُرُكَ وَلَا نَكْفُرُكَ وَنَخْلَعُ وَنَتْرُكُ مَنْ يَفْجُرُكَ ۗ اَللّٰهُمَّ إِيَّاكَ نَعْبُدُ وَلَكَ نُصَلِّيْ وَنَسْجُدُ وَإِلَيْكَ نَسْعٰى وَنَحْفِدُ وَنَرْجُوْ رَحْمَتَكَ وَنَخْشٰى عَذَابَكَ إِنَّ عَذَابَكَ بِالْكُفَّارِ مُلْحِقٌ

O Allah! We seek Your help and forgiveness. We believe in You and rely upon You. We praise and thank You. We are not unthankful to You. We reject and leave him who disobeys You. O Allah! We worship You alone and pray and prostrate before You. We turn towards You and hope for Your mercy and we fear Your punishment, Your punishment is for the disbelievers.

THE MUSLIM CREED

A Muslim must believe in the following things as being true and real: Almighty Allah, His Angels, His Prophets, His Holy Books, the Life Hereafter, Predestination & Resurrection. These are beautifully summarised in Al-Iman Al-Muffasal.

The Muslim Creed — اَلْإِيْمَانُ الْمُفَصَّلُ

اٰمَنْتُ بِاللهِ وَمَلٰئِكَتِهِ وَكُتُبِهِ وَرُسُلِهِ وَالْيَوْمِ الْاٰخِرِ وَالْقَدَرِ خَيْرِهٖ وَشَرِّهٖ مِنَ اللهِ تَعَالٰى وَالْبَعْثِ بَعْدَ الْمَوْتِ

I believe in Allah Almighty, and His Angels, His Books, His Messengers, the Day of Judgement, predestination, all good and bad is from Allah and in the life hereafter.

Brief Description of the Creed — اَلْإِيْمَانُ الْمُجْمَلُ

اٰمَنْتُ بِاللهِ كَمَا هُوَ بِأَسْمَآئِهٖ وَصِفَاتِهٖ وَقَبِلْتُ جَمِيْعَ أَحْكَامِهٖ إِقْرَارٌ بِاللِّسَانِ وَتَصْدِيْقٌ بِالْقَلْبِ

I believe in Allah as described by His names and attributes and I have accepted all His commandments whilst proclaiming with the tongue and affirming it with the heart.

THE SIX HOLY WORDS

The First Holy Word: The Pure Word

لَآ إِلٰهَ إِلَّا اللهُ مُحَمَّدٌ رَّسُوْلُ اللهِ

There is no god but Allah, Muhammad is the Messenger of Allah.

The Second Holy Word: The Declaration of Faith

أَشْهَدُ أَنْ لَّآ إِلٰهَ إِلَّا اللهُ وَحْدَهُ لَا شَرِيْكَ لَهُ وَأَشْهَدُ أَنَّ مُحَمَّدًا عَبْدُهُ وَرَسُوْلُهُ

I bear witness that there is no god but Allah, He is alone and has no partner and I bear witness that Muhammad is His servant and messenger.

The Third Holy Word: The Praise

سُبْحَانَ اللهِ وَالْحَمْدُ لِلّٰهِ وَلَا إِلٰهَ إِلَّا اللهُ وَاللهُ أَكْبَرُ وَلَا حَوْلَ وَلَا قُوَّةَ إِلَّا بِاللهِ الْعَلِيِّ الْعَظِيْمِ

Glory be to Allah and all Praise is for Allah and there is no god but Allah and Allah is the Greatest. There is no strength and power except that of Allah, the Exalted, the Greatest.

THE SIX HOLY WORDS

The Fourth Holy Word: Oneness of Allah

لَاۤ إِلٰهَ إِلَّا اللهُ وَحْدَهُ لَا شَرِيْكَ لَهُ، لَهُ الْمُلْكُ وَلَهُ الْحَمْدُ يُحْيِي وَيُمِيْتُ وَهُوَ حَيٌّ لَّا يَمُوْتُ أَبَدًا أَبَدًا ذُو الْجَلَالِ وَالْإِكْرَامِ بِيَدِهِ الْخَيْرُ وَهُوَ عَلٰى كُلِّ شَىْءٍ قَدِيْرٌ

There is no god except Allah, He is alone and has no partner, to Him belongs the kingdom and all praise. He gives life and death and is ever alive and will never die. The Majestic and Blessed One, in His hands (authority) is all goodness, and He has power over everything.

The Fifth Holy Word: Seeking Forgiveness

أَسْتَغْفِرُ اللهَ رَبِّىْ مِنْ كُلِّ ذَنْبٍ أَذْنَبْتُهُ عَمْدًا اَوْ خَطَاءً سِرًّا أَوْ عَلَانِيَةً وَّأَتُوْبُ إِلَيْهِ مِنَ الذَّنْبِ الَّذِىْ أَعْلَمُ وَمِنَ الذَّنْبِ الَّذِىْ لَا أَعْلَمُ إِنَّكَ أَنْتَ عَلَّامُ الْغُيُوْبِ وَسَتَّارُ الْعُيُوْبِ وَغَفَّارُ الذُّنُوْبِ وَلَا حَوْلَ وَلَا قُوَّةَ إِلَّا بِاللهِ الْعَلِىِّ الْعَظِيْمِ

O my Lord! I seek forgiveness for all the sins I have committed knowingly or mistakenly, secretly or openly and I repent from sins that I am aware of and from the sins that I am unaware of. You are the Knower of all secrets, the Concealer of all faults and the Forgiver of all sins. And there is no strength and power except that of Allah, the Exalted and the Greatest.

THE SIX HOLY WORDS

The Sixth Holy Word: The Rejection of Disbelief

اَللّٰهُمَّ إِنِّىْ أَعُوْذُ بِكَ مِنْ أَنْ أُشْرِكَ بِكَ شَيْئاً وَّ أَنَا أَعْلَمُ بِهٖ وَأَسْتَغْفِرُكَ لِمَا لَآ أَعْلَمُ بِهٖ تُبْتُ عَنْهُ وَتَبَرَّأْتُ مِنَ الْكُفْرِ وَالشِّرْكِ وَالْكِذْبِ وَالْغِيْبَةِ وَالْبِدْعَةِ وَالنَّمِيْمَةِ وَالْفَوَاحِشِ وَالْبُهْتَانِ وَالْمَعَاصِىْ كُلِّهَا وَأَسْلَمْتُ وَأَقُوْلُ لَا إِلٰهَ إِلَّا اللهُ مُحَمَّدٌ رَّسُوْلُ اللهِ

O Allah! I seek Your refuge from associating anything with You knowingly, and seek Your forgiveness for what I do not know. I have repented from it and I have freed myself from disbelief, idolatry, lying, backbiting, bad innovations, gossiping, indecency, accusations and all sins. I have submitted and I say there is no god but Allah, Muhammad is the Messenger of Allah.

20 GLORIOUS SURAHS OF THE QURAN

Surah 95: At-Teen (The Fig)

In the name of Allah, the Kind, the Caring.

How wonderful is the human physique?
¹By the fig, by the olive, ²by Mount Sinai ³and this safe city. ⁴We created humans in the most beautiful form, ⁵then reduced them to the lowest of the lows, due to disobedience, ⁶except those who believed and performed honourable deeds; they shall have a never-ending reward. ⁷So after knowing this what makes you deny Judgement Day? ⁸Isn't Allah the most Just Judge?

(Translation From: The Majestic Quran)

20 GLORIOUS SURAHS OF THE QURAN

Surah 96: Alaq (The Clot of Blood)

بِسْمِ اللهِ الرَّحْمٰنِ الرَّحِيْمِ

اِقْرَأْ بِاسْمِ رَبِّكَ الَّذِيْ خَلَقَ ۚ﴿١﴾ خَلَقَ الْاِنْسَانَ مِنْ عَلَقٍ ۚ﴿٢﴾ اِقْرَأْ وَرَبُّكَ الْاَكْرَمُ ۙ﴿٣﴾ الَّذِيْ عَلَّمَ بِالْقَلَمِ ۙ﴿٤﴾ عَلَّمَ الْاِنْسَانَ مَا لَمْ يَعْلَمْ ؕ﴿٥﴾ كَلَّا اِنَّ الْاِنْسَانَ لَيَطْغٰىٓ ۙ﴿٦﴾ اَنْ رَّاٰهُ اسْتَغْنٰى ؕ﴿٧﴾ اِنَّ اِلٰى رَبِّكَ الرُّجْعٰى ؕ﴿٨﴾ اَرَاَيْتَ الَّذِيْ يَنْهٰى ۙ﴿٩﴾ عَبْدًا اِذَا صَلّٰى ؕ﴿١٠﴾ اَرَاَيْتَ اِنْ كَانَ عَلَى الْهُدٰىٓ ۙ﴿١١﴾ اَوْ اَمَرَ بِالتَّقْوٰى ؕ﴿١٢﴾ اَرَاَيْتَ اِنْ كَذَّبَ وَتَوَلّٰى ؕ﴿١٣﴾ اَلَمْ يَعْلَمْ بِاَنَّ اللهَ يَرٰى ؕ﴿١٤﴾ كَلَّا لَئِنْ لَّمْ يَنْتَهِ ەۙ لَنَسْفَعًۢا بِالنَّاصِيَةِ ۙ﴿١٥﴾ نَاصِيَةٍ كَاذِبَةٍ خَاطِئَةٍ ۚ﴿١٦﴾ فَلْيَدْعُ نَادِيَهٗ ۙ﴿١٧﴾ سَنَدْعُ الزَّبَانِيَةَ ۙ﴿١٨﴾ كَلَّا ؕ لَا تُطِعْهُ وَاسْجُدْ وَاقْتَرِبْ ۩﴿١٩﴾

20 GLORIOUS SURAHS OF THE QURAN

Surah 96: Alaq (The Clot of Blood)

In the name of Allah, the Kind, the Caring.

The first revelation
¹Recite in the name of your Lord Who created, ²created humans from clustered germ-cells. ³Recite! "Your Lord is the most Generous", ⁴Who taught with the Pen, ⁵He taught humans what they didn't know.

Abu Jahl is warned of dreadful consequences
⁶But humans go beyond boundaries of Allah, ⁷considering themselves to be self-sufficient. ⁸Yet the final return is to your Lord. ⁹Have you seen the one who stops ¹⁰a servant of Ours from praying? ¹¹Don't you realise he is rightly guided, ¹²and issues commands based on fear of Allah? ¹³Have you considered, when he denies the truth and turns away, ¹⁴doesn't he know Allah sees everything? ¹⁵No! If he doesn't end this behaviour, We shall drag him by the forelock, ¹⁶that lying and sinful forelock. ¹⁷So let him call out to his supporters; ¹⁸We shall summon the angel guards at the gates of Hell to take care of him. ¹⁹No! Don't follow him, Prophet, but prostrate before Us and draw ever closer.

20 GLORIOUS SURAHS OF THE QURAN

Surah 97: Al-Qadar (The Night of Destiny)

In the name of Allah, the Kind, the Caring.

The Night of Power
¹We sent down the Quran on the Night of Destiny, ²and what can explain the Night of Destiny to you? ³The Night of Destiny is better than one thousand months; ⁴the angels and the Spirit, Jibreel, come down by the order of their Lord, bringing with them each person's destiny. ⁵Peace descends everywhere until the break of the dawn.

20 GLORIOUS SURAHS OF THE QURAN

Surah 98: Al-Biyyanah (The Clear Proof)

لَمْ يَكُنِ الَّذِينَ كَفَرُوا مِنْ أَهْلِ الْكِتَٰبِ وَالْمُشْرِكِينَ مُنفَكِّينَ حَتَّىٰ تَأْتِيَهُمُ الْبَيِّنَةُ ۝ رَسُولٌ مِّنَ اللَّهِ يَتْلُوا۟ صُحُفًا مُّطَهَّرَةً ۝ فِيهَا كُتُبٌ قَيِّمَةٌ ۝ وَمَا تَفَرَّقَ الَّذِينَ أُوتُوا الْكِتَٰبَ إِلَّا مِنۢ بَعْدِ مَا جَاءَتْهُمُ الْبَيِّنَةُ ۝ وَمَا أُمِرُوا إِلَّا لِيَعْبُدُوا اللَّهَ مُخْلِصِينَ لَهُ الدِّينَ حُنَفَاءَ وَيُقِيمُوا الصَّلَوٰةَ وَيُؤْتُوا الزَّكَوٰةَ ۚ وَذَٰلِكَ دِينُ الْقَيِّمَةِ ۝ إِنَّ الَّذِينَ كَفَرُوا مِنْ أَهْلِ الْكِتَٰبِ وَالْمُشْرِكِينَ فِي نَارِ جَهَنَّمَ خَٰلِدِينَ فِيهَا ۚ أُو۟لَٰٓئِكَ هُمْ شَرُّ الْبَرِيَّةِ ۝ إِنَّ الَّذِينَ ءَامَنُوا وَعَمِلُوا الصَّٰلِحَٰتِ أُو۟لَٰٓئِكَ هُمْ خَيْرُ الْبَرِيَّةِ ۝ جَزَاؤُهُمْ عِندَ رَبِّهِمْ جَنَّٰتُ عَدْنٍ تَجْرِى مِن تَحْتِهَا الْأَنْهَٰرُ خَٰلِدِينَ فِيهَا أَبَدًا ۖ رَضِيَ اللَّهُ عَنْهُمْ وَرَضُوا عَنْهُ ۚ ذَٰلِكَ لِمَنْ خَشِيَ رَبَّهُۥ ۝

20 GLORIOUS SURAHS OF THE QURAN

Surah 98: Al-Biyyanah (The Clear Proof)

In the name of Allah, the Kind, the Caring.

People are given an opportunity before being condemned
[1] The disbelievers among the People of the Book and the idolaters were not condemned until the clear proof had come to them – [2] the Messenger of Allah recited pages of pure teachings from the Quran, [3] containing clear commandments. [4] Those given the Book became divided after the clear proof had come to them. [5] They were commanded: worship Allah sincerely, turn away from false gods, establish the prayer, and pay the Zakat. That is the religion of truth. [6] The disbelievers from the People of The Book and the idolaters will be in the Hell-Fire forever. These are the worst of the creatures.

Believers are richly rewarded
[7] The believers who did righteous works are the best of the creatures. [8] Their reward is with the Lord: Gardens of Eden beneath which rivers flow; they will live there forever. Allah is pleased with them, and they're pleased with Him. That's for the one who fears His Lord.

20 GLORIOUS SURAHS OF THE QURAN

Surah 99: Zalzalah (The Earthquake)

In the name of Allah, the Kind, the Caring.

The Divine Justice

¹When the Earth is shaken violently, ²it will throw up its burden; ³people will ask, "What's the matter with her?" ⁴That Day, it will tell all its news, ⁵inspired by her Lord. ⁶That Day, people will come separately in groups to be shown their deeds. ⁷So, anyone who did an atom's weight of good will see it. ⁸And anyone who did an atom's weight of evil will see it too.

20 GLORIOUS SURAHS OF THE QURAN

Surah 100: Adiyat (The War Horses)

In the name of Allah, the Kind, the Caring.

The unthankfulness of humans

¹By the snorting war horses, ²their hooves striking sparks, ³charging in dawn raids ⁴scattering dust clouds ⁵then dashing into the centre of the enemy. ⁶Human beings are most unthankful to His Lord. ⁷He is a witness to this, ⁸and passionately loves wealth. ⁹Doesn't he know everything in the graves will be thrown out, ¹⁰and the secrets of hearts will be revealed? ¹¹That Day their Lord will be aware of them.

20 GLORIOUS SURAHS OF THE QURAN

Surah 101: Qariah (The Sudden Calamity)

In the name of Allah, the Kind, the Caring.

Good deeds are the basis of success

¹The Sudden Calamity! ²What is the Sudden Calamity? ³What can explain the reality of the Sudden Calamity to you? ⁴The Day when people will look lost, like scattered moths, ⁵and the mountains will sway like fluffy wool. ⁶So the one who has heavy scales of deeds ⁷will have a happy life. ⁸But the one who has light scales of deeds ⁹his home will be a bottomless Pit. ¹⁰What can explain what it looks like to you? ¹¹A Blazing Fire!

20 GLORIOUS SURAHS OF THE QURAN

Surah 102: Takathur (The Competition for More and More)

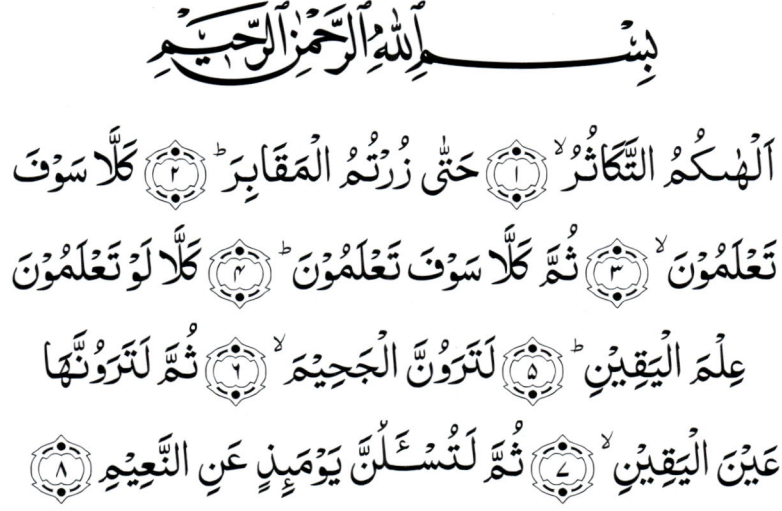

In the name of Allah, the Kind, the Caring.

Human greed
¹The competition for more and more wealth preoccupied you, ²until you went down in your graves. ³Surely, you will know; ⁴Eventually you will understand. ⁵If only you had knowledge of certainty. ⁶You will certainly see Hell; ⁷you will see it with the eye of certainty; ⁸that Day, you will be questioned about all the gifts.

20 GLORIOUS SURAHS OF THE QURAN

Surah 103: Asr (The Age)

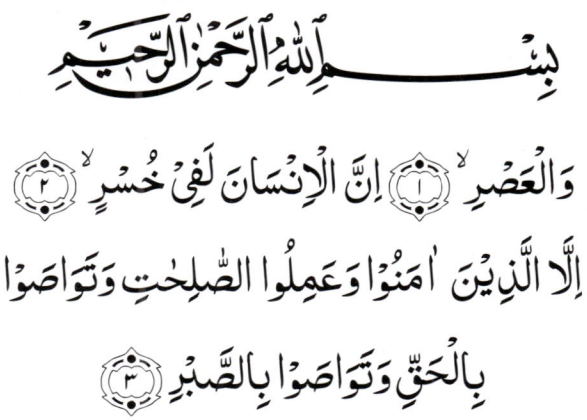

In the name of Allah, the Kind, the Caring.

Humans are at a loss unless they are righteous

By the age, ²humans are at a loss, ³except the believers who are righteous, and encourage each other to be truthful and patient.

20 GLORIOUS SURAHS OF THE QURAN

Surah 104: Humazah (The Faultfinder)

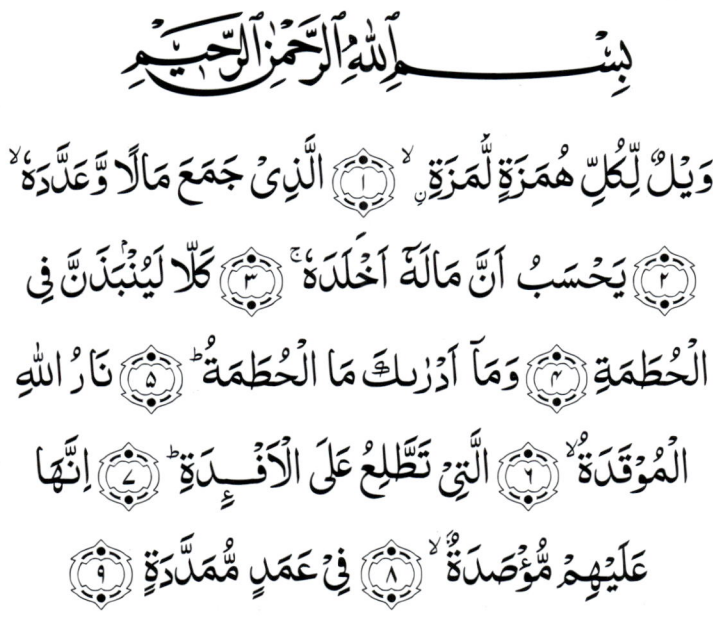

In the name of Allah, the Kind, the Caring.

Beware of the idolisation of wealth

[1] Wretched is every backbiting fault-finder, [2] who gathers wealth and counts it over and over, [3] thinking his wealth will make him live forever. [4] No, he will be thrown into the Crusher! [5] And what can explain to you what the Crusher is? [6] Allah's blazing Fire, [7] which rises over their hearts. [8] Indeed, it is closed over them from all sides, [9] flames stretching out in columns.

20 GLORIOUS SURAHS OF THE QURAN

Surah 105: Al-Fil (The Elephant)

In the name of Allah, the Kind, the Caring.

The defeat of Abraha

Have you not seen how your Lord dealt with the army of the elephant? ²Didn't He smash their plan? ³When He sent a flock of birds against them, ⁴they pelted them with flint-stones. ⁵So, He turned them into what looked like chewed hay.

20 GLORIOUS SURAHS OF THE QURAN

Surah 106: Quraysh (The Tribe of Quraysh)

In the name of Allah, the Kind, the Caring.

The Quraysh were safe

¹For the Quraysh's feeling of security – ²their security in the winter and summer journeys. ³So, they should worship the Lord of this house, the Kaaba, ⁴Who feeds them, protects from famine and gives them safety from fear.

20 GLORIOUS SURAHS OF THE QURAN

Surah 107: Al-Ma'un (Small Kindness)

In the name of Allah, the Kind, the Caring.

Small kindnesses

Have you seen the person who denies the Judgement? ²He treats an orphan roughly, ³and doesn't feel the urge to feed the needy. ⁴So, ruined are the worshippers ⁵who are forgetful of their prayers, ⁶who merely show off, ⁷and even stop doing small kindnesses.

20 GLORIOUS SURAHS OF THE QURAN

Surah 108: Al-Kawthar (The Abundance)

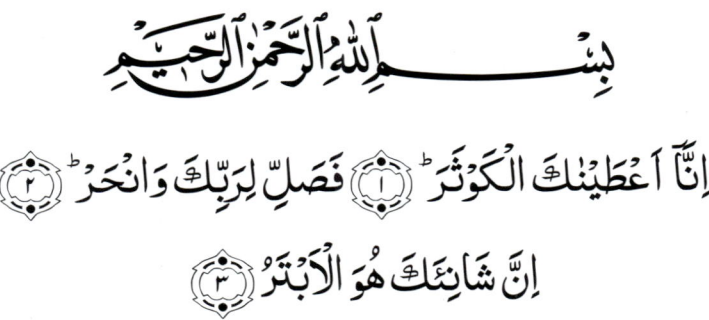

In the name of Allah, the Kind, the Caring.

The Prophet will not be cut off; his enemies will

¹We gave everything in abundance to you, ²so, pray to your Lord and make a sacrifice. ³Your enemy will be finished, cut off.

20 GLORIOUS SURAHS OF THE QURAN

Surah 109: Al-Kafirun (The Disbelievers)

In the name of Allah, the Kind, the Caring.

Co-existence of religions

Say: "Disbelievers, ²I don't worship what you worship, ³neither are you worshippers of what I worship. ⁴Nor will I be a worshipper of what you worship, ⁵neither will you be worshippers of what I worship. ⁶For you is your religion, and for me is mine."

20 GLORIOUS SURAHS OF THE QURAN

Surah 110: Al-Nasr (The Help)

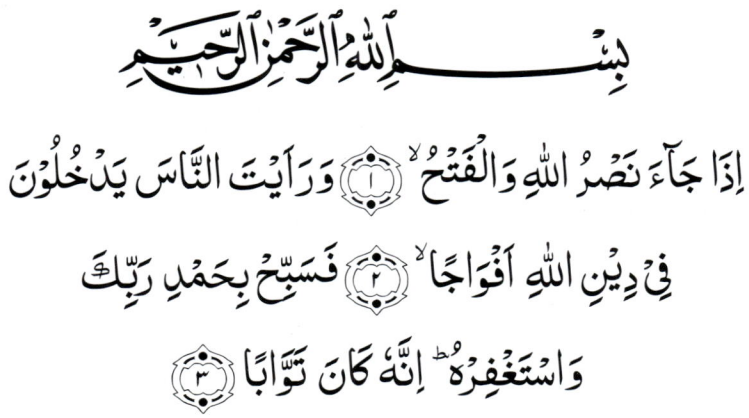

In the name of Allah, the Kind, the Caring.

Be grateful in times of success

¹When Allah's help and the victory comes ²and you see masses of people entering Allah's religion, ³then glorify and praise Your Lord, and seek His forgiveness. He is ever ready to accept repentance.

20 GLORIOUS SURAHS OF THE QURAN

Surah 111: Al-Lahab (The Flame)

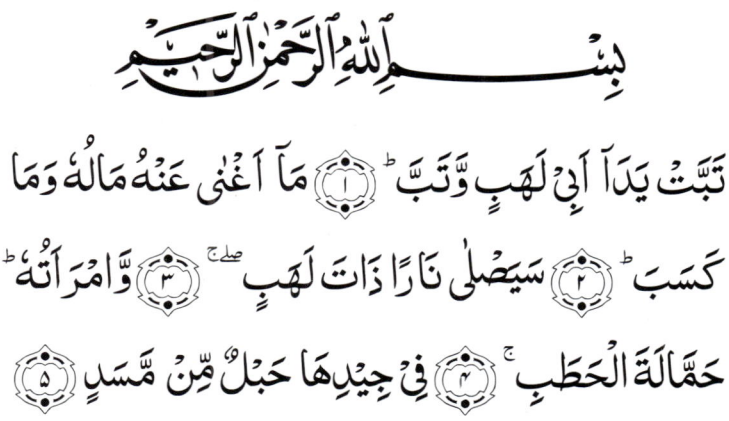

In the name of Allah, the Kind, the Caring.

Abu Lahab will be punished

Abu Lahab's hands are broken, he's ruined. ²Neither his wealth nor his achievements will help him. ³Soon he will enter the Flaming Fire; ⁴so will his wife, the firewood-carrier – ⁵she will have a rope of palm-fibre around her neck.

20 GLORIOUS SURAHS OF THE QURAN

Surah 112: Al-Ikhlas (Sincere Faith)

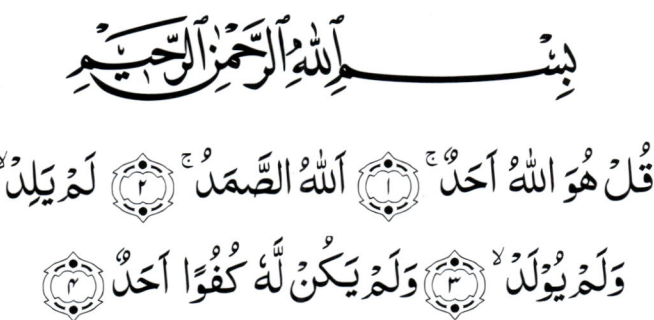

In the name of Allah, the Kind, the Caring.

Allah, the One

¹Say: "He is Allah, the One, ²Allah the Eternal. ³He is not a father nor a son. ⁴None is equal to Him."

20 GLORIOUS SURAHS OF THE QURAN

Surah 113: Al-Falaq (The Daybreak)

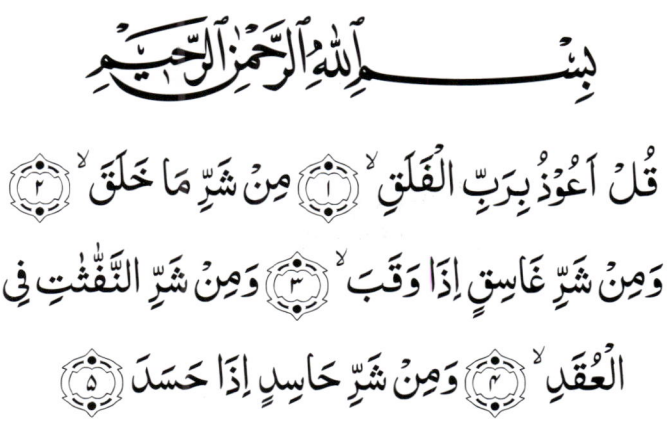

In the name of Allah, the Kind, the Caring.

Seek refuge with Allah

Say: "I seek refuge in the Lord of the daybreak, ²from the harm of all His creation, ³from the harm of the ever-darkening night, ⁴from the harm of witches who blow on knots, ⁵and from the harm of a jealous person when jealous."

20 GLORIOUS SURAHS OF THE QURAN

Surah 114: Al-Nas (The People)

In the name of Allah, the Kind, the Caring.

Seek Allah's refuge from evil

¹Say: "I seek refuge in the Lord of the people, ²the King of the people, ³the God of the people, ⁴from the evil of the sneaking whisperer, ⁵who whispers into people's hearts and minds, ⁶from among the jinn or the people."

Now that you have finished learning all the rules required to read the Quran correctly, you are now ready to begin the journey of reading Allah's book.

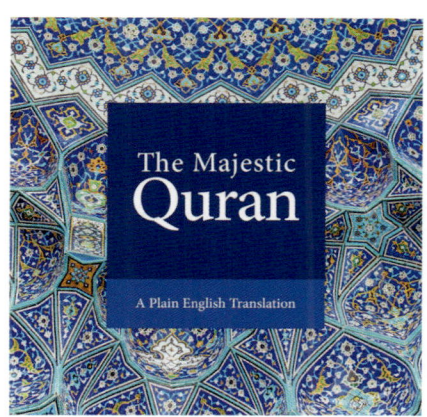

www.majesticquran.co.uk

NOTES

NOTES

NOTES